OTHER BOOKS BY

fragile: a memoir.
Red Mountain Press, 2015.

The Complete Poems of Catullus: An Annotated Translation.
Cambridge University Press, 2015

Birdwatching in Wartime.
Carnegie Mellon University Press, 2009

From the Fishouse: An Anthology of Poems that Sing, Rhyme,
Resound, Syncopate, Alliterate, and Just Plain Sound Great.
Persea Books, 2009

Renovation.
Carnegie Mellon University Press, 2005

The Country of Lost Sons.
Parlor Press, 2004

The Halo Brace.
Birch Brook Press, 1998

salmonpoetry

The Belfast Notebooks

Poems & Prose

JEFFREY THOMSON

Published in 2017 by
Salmon Poetry
Cliffs of Moher, County Clare, Ireland
Website: www.salmonpoetry.com
Email: info@salmonpoetry.com

ISBN 978-1-910669-71-6

COVER IMAGE: Belfast skyline in black watercolor
© Domiciano Pablo Romero Franco
COVER DESIGN & TYPESETTING: *Siobhán Hutson*
Printed in Ireland by Sprint Print

for the teachers and students
of the Seamus Heaney Poetry Center

Acknowledgments

Poems from this manuscript appeared in the following places, some in slightly different form. My thanks to the editors and readers of all these journals and anthologies.

"New Faces of Belfast." *AGNI*
"Led Zeppelin Debuts 'Stairway to Heaven,' Ulster Hall, March 5, 1971,"
"Van Morrison Performs with his daughter: Odyssey Auditorium,
    Belfast" & "Rain, or a local poet long gone returns."
    Beloit Poetry Journal
"Self-portrait in Nine Generations." *Many Mountains Moving*
"Silence" and "Surfing Dunfagnaghy: Donegal, Ireland." *Puerto del Sol*
"Slash City," "The Arab Baths in Ronda," and "El Café a la Esquina
    de Agua y Vida." *Connotation Press*
"Watercolor Painting Class" & "The Rolling Stones Visit the Cave of
    Hercules, 1967, Morocco." *The Birmingham Poetry Review*
"Certain things here are quietly American" & "Archeology." *Terrain.org*
"DaVinci Drawings in the Ulster Museum" & "Sleeping Through It."
    The Maine Review
"Artists Sketching in the White Mountains" & "Two Northern Crows."
    ISLE
"Samson and Goliath." *Other Countries: Contemporary Poets Rewiring History*
"For the Blind Man in the Basilica di Santa Croce, Florence."
    Academy of American Poets, Poem-a-Day, 9/24/15.
    www.poets.org/poetsorg/poem/blind-man-basilica-di-santa-croce-florence

Many of the poems here also appeared in a limited-edition chapbook, *The New Faces of Belfast*, from Anchor & Plume Press, 2015. Thanks to Amanda Mays for her support and her wise-words and sharp eyes.

Additional thanks are due to many people who helped the writing of this book in myriad ways: Christian Barter, for being an ever-generous and critical reader; Connie Voisne, for being there and being twice the teacher I am; Sinéad and Ciaran, for lighting the way; and, as always, Jennifer and Julian, for coming with me. And for those here named and unnamed—the friends and colleagues, the poets and the readers, the teachers and the students—who made the wounds of Belfast into wonder.

Contents

Belfast
is many

places then
as now

all lie
in ruins

and
it is

as much
as I can do

to save
even one

from oblivion.

~ Ciaran Carson

Led Zeppelin Debuts "Stairway to Heaven," Ulster Hall, March 5, 1971

> *...more than 900 were killed that night*
> *and half the homes in Belfast destroyed.*
> ~ BBC

The crowd waits, ready to burst into anything but this
slow-motion wreck of an intro they've never heard before

with its swaying guitar and that recorder floating
out of the dark like Irish pipes, and now some jostle

to the bar in the back, talking over the top of
this strange *lady who's sure all that glitters is gold*

and into the white faces on the tops of their pints,
while one girl—spattered with paisley and red beads

like stopped droplets of blood—sways back and forth
before the stage (the tempo and the reefer in perfect

harmony now) and no longer wonders about
this man with blunt hands and manners short

as his hair, this man she recently started thinking of
as her love, no longer wonders when he will return

to put his arms around her in the clumsy way
she finds endearing but suspects that—if it lasts—

she will come to loathe, and then the lights drop
and Plant sweeps the golden blitz of his hair

across his eyes in echo of the gold leaf sparkling
across the ceiling like the small and distant fires

of homes burning in the hills all around him
as if it is Easter Tuesday, 1941, again, and

the American soldiers whose children will gather
like druids around any turntable playing this song

are sudden darkness and silence
as air-raid sirens squeal up into the distant hills,

the city unprepared for it (no searchlights accusing
the cloud-speckled sky, no chuff of anti-aircraft)

and because there is nothing to be done and nowhere
to go, Delia Murphy, up on stage in chiffon and lace

as bombs begin their soft percussion
in the distance, says, "We're not going anywhere,"

and drops into "Bye Bye Blackbird" as one soldier
gathers the small bouquet of an Irish girl in his arms

and swings her onto the bare runway of the dance floor—
this floor that will collapse twice in years to come

beneath dancers pounding their lives into it with all
the rhythm the small hammers of their feet can manage,

but not this night, no, not tonight—and now other
soldiers drop their need, their dread urgency

to do *something* and follow his lead, gathering
their own girls from the garden of faces along the wall

and soon the floor is swirling and Murphy is singing,
Make my bed and light the light, I'll be home late tonight,

bombs dropping across the city from a flotilla of diesel
and gear, dropping down alleyways carved into the air,

and they dance on into the night, hour after hour
as clouds and blaze swirl up throughout the city

like flirtatious color gels spinning paisley and psychodelia
across the scene, Plant picking up the tempo now,

buckets of drumbeats dropped at his feet, Page's guitar
rising on the upbeats, and the lights pound

and the sound rises and the crowd finally engages,
boys returning from the bar in waves like aircraft

coasting above a defenseless, darkened city and
when he does return and slide his arms around her,

his hands meaty as peat, she will smile and think him
wonderful, aware only of his hands and the music

and the ripe crush of the crescendo as it breaks
across them both, together there on that fragile floor,

not knowing, of course, that he will die in McGurk's
in December of that very year, die beneath a wall

brought down by another bomb, brought down
out of some terrible and ongoing heaven.

New Faces of Belfast

It's 1972, the year the Ambassador finally
closes, the theater's cathedral arches rigid
in the fall's afternoon gloom, asphalt a small
galaxy of shattered glass and graffiti duct-
working walls, and *What's New Pussycat?*
still sparkles on the marquee—as if
the world's a many-roomed mansion split
between paisley and pinstripe, a bacchanal
and carnival that will not last the night—

but there is this question of the new faces
that appeared overnight smeared on plywood
sheeting locking in the construction site
next door, these new faces of Belfast,
wanted posters like promos for a film yet
to come starring Murphy and the leaders
of the Shankill Butchers horse-brushed
to the wall with a glue of broken glass
to separate the blood from a man's hands
should he try and pull them from the wall;

these faces tell a story that will take years
to finish, a story called abduction and extremity,
a story called hard man and kneecapper,
a story called trouble. Many will die wearing
shirts of their own blood when they've heard it,
but today we know what we know and
it is little. Today the marquee's lights trickle
on merrily and the eyes of the posters mark
dark knots in the wood. Today jackdaws
lift their gray hoods above the roofline
and night lies down along the Falls Road.

Of Brian Boru, the first King of Ireland, it is said,

that his tomb's black and gold placard shines
beneath a mottled sky with the dull light
of all things once vital and daffodils besiege
the cathedral where two-toned, northern crows

jag and haw in the oak. That much is true.
Bróðir killed him in his tent, it is said,
as Brian prayed after the Battle of Clontarf,
the blade joining his back to the ground.

It is said, too, that Brian died fighting Bróðir
man-to-man on Good Friday, his armor shining
like that rarest of suns here in Armagh, a sun
that wrestles clouds aside and spears

the earth with a pole of light. It is also said
that Brian died in his sleep in the night,
the way rain comes down from the sky now—
its tranquility a blessing—the great shipwreck

of battle gathered around his tent. Then, Brian
was the first to gather all the clans together
around the fire beneath the lonely sermon of
a similar rain in hope that the sun might find a way

through the clouds the way a lone ship arrives
across an open sea to an island green and new:
buds open in time-lapse across the surrounding
Mournes and those mountains gather like the ships

of some invading army as wind accumulates
in the raised sails of the trees. No one knows,
it is said, if Brian truly lies here.
In truth, no one knows anything but the rain

comes harder now and drives the day south and we descend
to find a peat fire and the black welcome of pints
in the Hole in the Wall, the oldest pub in Armagh, it is said,
with windows like portholes looking out on an ocean of sky.

Certain things here are quietly American

~ Derek Walcott

The fence and wall, the town divided
the way a clock is divided by time
as the Lough cuts the one o'clock hour
from its face. All the missing trains.
Parking lots chock-a-block by eight
surrounding savage, seventies architecture
where foxglove breaks pavement with
a will unlike the old Irish backstory.
The Apple Store shining like the church
of all things modern. Mute factories
brittle with webs of broken windows
where workers once walked down to
from Belfast with overalls and pails
then stepped up late afternoon to the rail
for a few jars before slumping uphill
home in the long graying of dusk to wives
whose day was made of muscling water
into flax at the river's edge. Dockyards
abandoned with the want of urban space,
piers slapped by the seawater wake
tossed by the hulking ferry that glows white
as it churns up the lough. Dog-faced seals
that raise their untroubled heads to watch
the ship pass through the gunmetal gap
the sea plows through these Antrim hills,
fields divided stone by stone on either shore.

Van Morrison Performs "Sometimes We Cry" with his Daughter, Odyssey Arena, Belfast

cab driver asks, not really asking, as we're driving through Shaftsbury Square and the collapse of old churches down to this new Odyssey which hovers like a lit ship beside the shore.

He forgets where he comes from, so he does, the driver continues as we pass an old wall camouflaged by a mural of red hands that flank a masked gunman. This wall painted with scarlet fists like all the small roses of rage. This wall that warns— YOU ARE NOW ENTERING LOYALIST SANDY ROW—as the Union Jacks accumulate along the street beneath the rain like questions.

In the gauzy wasteland of myth one man wanted this island so desperately that he separated his hand from his arm with his own sword and heaved the flaccid crab of it from his ship to the rocky shore to win the race to first put skin on Ulster, so now red hands mark a bloody map spattered on buildings across the city.

Inside the Odyssey, by the time his daughter slides out from behind the risers to sing "Sometime We Cry," a song that now sounds to me like the true duet of the North, Van's easy Irish soul has come and gone like a home left long ago. What's left is raw. They stand together, both of them downstage like two worlds joined: her voice gossamer as a thin cloud in the long blue collapse of day over the Lough added to the brackish, black estuary of his jazz growl.

The piano builds a pier out across the water for them to cross and they wander out to where the sunrise of their voices builds an island in the air and the surf bothers the bird-churned shore and the unending oak forest, a perpetual home glossed with the lace of breaking waves.

But back here in Belfast, the lough is colored with the sky's gray flannel and small gardens struggle beside the row houses—new paint covering whitewash mottled like a map of an old, old world. Stones assemble along the shore, stones that writhe with hundreds of crabs like a collection of severed hands, and all the stars are hidden.

They finish the song and wave to us in front of the dark altar of the drums as the rough surf of applause beats down on them. The past has become its own Ithaca and that island on the horizon hovers still. Their two hands join at the edge of the stage, lit up as if they are wearing history's bloody glove and the future's long white dress.

Man vs. Wild

Magnus Bare Legs breached the green wall
of Ireland and unlocked the inner core
of Ulster here in Strangford where my son

is filming a video of himself as Bear Gryls,
who—by name alone—should've been one
of the Vikings who first built this sweetpastoral

of a Irish town: row houses and the harbor,
tower of blocked stone overseeing the power
of the sea as it invades the channel daily.

Past the village and up along the lough,
a green sheen of Spring holds on despite
the earliness of the year. He hold his arm

out ahead of him and says, *I have been dropped off
here in the wild with nothing but a camera
and this crappy English accent.* Ash saplings

netted with fresh ivy. Stone walls and the olive
running of the hedgerows. The sea slick
with the multiple grays of the sky

and stone. He says, *I have found an object
that can be very useful in the wild. It's called a stick.*
His blond hair flops wild across his eyes.

Here, the lough floods into the country like a long rift
of danger that Magnus and his bear-clad followed
moonless north to the monastery at Nendrum—

everyone asleep beneath their skins. He climbs
the branches of a hawthorn hanging low and says,
I have found a place to safely spend the night, in this tree.

A tree is like a big stick. The three concentric cashels
of dry stone were not enough to save them.
Now the round tower only remains,

a ruined church with a sun-dial,
and the graveyard. Our small-town
walk just begun, we've come back

the long way around, and he says,
It appears that I had my cell phone on me
the whole time and could have just called for help.

A blue tractor churns mud across the valley
toward homes that toss up veins of smoke from fires
warming neat seas of light around their hearths.

for Julian

Pole Dancing for Easter

In the Crown Saloon every pint gets poured with a shamrock curled in the white foam that floats on the ruby-black, and up the road the mad convergence of Shaftsbury Square bustles like a lake of light and traffic and beer—all the wild rumpus of a Belfast Friday night in Spring—but there is rain again beneath clouds speckled with the dull glitter of every possible gray. Rain that washes the pastoral of the North to a brutal pastel.

Rain's sodden gravity fills the Antrim hills beyond town and *Pole Dancing for Easter* bleats the neon sign in the window of the Viceroy Lounge because Christ died for the glitter spangling the chest of the girl on stage as she rides her pole in desperation and at the end of hope. Boys across the street play chicken with traffic and couples hump against wall of the V-Club.

Rain fills the Square and the road beyond, towards churches that fold in on themselves like umbrellas of brick. Bookies and taxi stands bark at each other across the slide and honk of evening traffic.

Rain charges live wires of neon on the pavement and with their tracksuits and liters of Strongbow line up along the Lagan beside the Clarence dock to piss into the river where the old canal's blocked up and the granite steps drop down into the water.

Rain fills the city inch by inch, like the cold sediment of history. Rain webs windows shut like bars. Rain as if the eternal emptying of the hosepipe of the Atlantic might finally soothe this wounded city, offer damp solace, the way that, up in Lavery's, the bartender with the scars across his arms he got when that parcel bomb went off in here so in so many years ago, pours Jaeger while my pint settles and then smiles damply as he goes again to get the mop to clean the water that's carried in on every foot from a rain that keeps on coming.

Stroke City

Here the police patrol in squads of seven—full military formation, one man on point and one woman sweeping, turning again to check her six—as I search for my family's Presbyterian Church. Locked-down walls built long ago frame the old town and the oak grove at the top that the city's named for. St. Columb's cathedral stands overwhelmed with Union Jacks for July as the Orange Order gatehouse supervises Bogside tenements where murals recall Bloody Sunday and Operation Motorman.

For a town nicknamed Stroke City—the slash between the English and the Irish, capitol and plantation, the eternal face-off and a city divided, town signs painted over again and again to read ~~LONDON~~/derry in a palimpsest of rage and repetition—all this makes sense.

Did I tell you that we came through here? My people, I mean. William, his name was, and he was planted like some kind of root stock the English hoped would spread, tenacious as ribbon grass, with the other Scots to control the last of the Irish chieftains. But what he found was Anne, a catholic wife from Donegal, and a city where neither were welcome.

When I find his Church, it's a minor thing. Might as well be a bank now. Doric columns and the high windows framing the façade beneath the glazed light of the late sun.

He would have seen the beginnings of it all—civil wars and a time called trouble—here on the Grand Parade where 14 sycamores (one each for the apprentice boys who locked a gate on the imminent Jacobite king) now line walls he walked between the Hangman's bastion and the Coward's where, when the siege went bad and even rats were scarce and the hides of horses tasted of slaughter, it was easiest to escape. But I see only a little.

William escaped, that's true and all I know, as the soldiers turn the corner ahead of me, cautious as cats, and sycamores drop thousands of tiny keys across the walls of the city, but I have returned in hope of finding a way in through the locked door of this story—how he must have walked with Anne, her hand resting on his arm, watching the sun break open clouds coming up out of the west and talking softly about a new world.

for my father, and his before him

Self-portrait in Nine Generations

William strides out of the Glasgow dusk,
long-legged in the summer light that only fails
late into the night, and then he gathers Anne,
his new wife, from Donegal, as if she were
a basket of fruit, a gift to bring to his new hosts,
and then he's here in Philadelphia (on paper
it seems so easy—we can ignore the three-month
thrashing in steerage, puking in the dripping dark)
and James will follow, a son, an American, he thinks,
after all there's revolution on every broadside
slapped against the board and batten, horse-
brushed with glue and he's a glass maker
whose specialty is floats for fishing nets—
the Gulf of Maine and the banks still roiling with cod
—and then just as suddenly there will be
Alexander who barely remembers William,
just a face edged with white, the smell of a pipe;
in fact, Alexander rarely thinks that far back
(he's still young and he's crossed the mountains
and there's a continent spread out before him
like the cloth spread across the table before
the plates of ox-tail and eels and the glazed-brown
goose are all laid down) and he has 9 children,
one of whom will be my great-great-great-grandfather,
and the print-shop he runs and Pennsylvania summers
go by so fast, and his children, who couldn't remember
if asked, spread out down river and over and that's
the past and this is a new world, and he's tired now—
the day's nearly done and the world's shrinking back
on him as his cataracts turn the world to milk and gauze
—and the almost-Scottish hills shoulder up into a sky
that carries the light of day long after the sun has set.

Watercolor Painting Class

Once a week above the rooftops
of Queen's Quarter—skylights
and chimneypots providing
the order the eye asks for—inside
an old girls school turned studio
where I was the youngest student
in a class retired long ago from
daily life in Belfast, checkpoints
and rifles, parades and old enemies
in mask and balaclava, pressure
of a city mounting toward the fires
of July, I worked my morning into
gardens of amaryllis and lily,
small pastoral welcome of geese
among outbuildings gray and streaked
as the rain crashed its shrapnel
on the exhaust vents for the kilns,
and, one day, as the sky crawled by
in its uniform of grim and somber,
I painted a close-up of the small star
of a sunflower with the all the colors
of the light I'd missed that winter,
filling the canvas with warm petals
of citron and blonde, champagne
and canary, and, at the heart of it all,
the black of the seedpod ready to explode.

The Pyre in Holywood

At the end of   the coastal path
miles of stone   and sea and wall
in this suburb   of small wounds
three stories of   rubbish stands
a grievance in   the roundabout
where the A1 turns   to follow
the coast   bloody fist
of a tower ready to   spark large
tindered pile   of resentment
Babel of pallets   and couches
lamps that failed   overwinter
in the dark   forest of rain
stacked auto-da-fé   waiting parade
body of rancor   middle finger
of blaze   and black
smoke statue   of wrath and
the unending past   gel of the year's
rage celebration   of the Orange
compass needle   pointing to fume
and thunder this   outcast this Jacob
this dream of angels   clothed in fury
ready to climb   a ladder of clouds
and a sky to burn themselves alive in

The Mona Lisa of Belfast

*The Mona Lisa is as famous for her weird ability to follow
you with her eyes as she is for her puzzling smile.*

~ Josh Clark

In this mural no vast landscape
swaddles into the distance,
no rivers braid a chalked savannah
of hills, no glossy lake, no road
toward a glimmer of pastoral ease.
In this mural a gunman with one eye
closed and the gun pointed right
at you, this enigma in a black hood,
this air of menace in the face
turned to face you, the flat motley
of camo, crossed Union Jacks,
and the raised rifle sight
that follows you through
the *sfumato* of Shankill field
(this orchard of ruin with
a no-man's land inside it).
Here there is just this message—
Quis Separabit?—clear as smashed
glass across this pitch and plain
as the red hand of Ulster,
bloody mitt not yet a fist,
this message and the gun sight
that follows you everywhere,
its simple, single eye tracking you
even as you try to leave through
rare sunlight speckling the open gate.

Da Vinci Drawings in the Ulster Museum

Ludovico Sforza demanded
a horse-warrior, a foursize
remembrance of his father,
Muzio, once called the Strong
but dead 20 long years,
so Leonardo first sketched
a towering mount rearing
over the cower and sob
of his defeated, the warrior's
arm thrown back for balance.

The face of young Leda he outlines
in haematite, red as henna, and
darkens with black chalk
on paper of pulped clothing.

Late in his life, da Vinci pencils
four sketches of the end of the world.

He spends more time on her hair,
complicated and intervwoven plaits,
the soft brillo of it,

Fire slithers through the molten sky
of the first as a fortress crumbles.

than he does on her eyes,
finishing them last, downcast
and soft, unguarded.

In the second, skeletons scramble
their graves and throng a roiling sky.

Not even da Vinci could
execute that vision, so
the model he cast at last

with clay brought up from
the distant Po in buckets
was 22 feet tall, with four
feet on the ground, striding
into the light of the life-after.

>   In the third, platoons of tiny bodies
>   char in judgment's wind.

>   *Leda unaware of all*
>   *that is to come,*

Leonardo hoarded bronze
to build the enormous horse.
But by the time he gathered
enough war was embarked on,
cannons worth more than horses.

>   In the last, a great ball of smoke and fire
>   goes astray across mountains and a boiling sea.

>   *that everything, even*
>   *the painting made*
>   *from this sketch,*
>   *will blaze and vanish.*

No statue was ever made
in those days before the French
soldiers arrived and turned his
clay model to buckets of wreckage
with their muskets, but
on cold mornings in Milan
in the courtyard at Palazzo Vecchio
that model horse cast out breath
when the sun brushed its flanks.

Two Northern Crows

Downpatrick

Up in the rare sky blue as a bruise,
blue as a song, blue as two oceans
coming together, blue as the irises
attached to the sides of the steps
leading up to a cathedral named
for a man once a slave who returned
to speak—as if in desperate need—
to those who had beaten him,
up in this brightening air, two birds
come together in midflight: one
hooded, the other like a man
with a blanket over his shoulders.
They come together with so much
of that desire that looks like rage
that they tumble through bare
hawthorns and collapse
daffodils beneath St. Patrick's
grave. They struggle in
the fresh grass, then each climbs
into an divided sphere, oblivious
to what connects them now,
a fine thread like a trip wire
that follows them through the sky.

Samson and Goliath

And all I ever learned of love
Was to shoot at someone who outdrew you.

~ Leonard Cohen

On the Lagan close by the weir in Belfast—
wounded city sewn together with
the chain-link stitching of fences—
the twin, canary brackets of Harland
and Wolff's huge shipyard gantry cranes
(named for giants overcome at the height
of their strength) line up like sutures and
the eye's needle draws out and through
to the patched-up hillsides beyond
as if sewing together the murky layerings

of history. You've heard the stories
I'm sure—Goliath who stood before
the Israelites like living thunder.
Goliath who looted the Ark, carried it
to the temple at Dagon. Whose head
was carted off to Jerusalem by David
as if to say: *You're next, motherfuckers!*
Samson who tied torches to the tails
of foxes and let them free in the fields of
the Philistines. Samson who was deceived
by Delilah, who was shorn and blinded,
and forced to grind grain. Samson who
brought the temple at Dagon down
upon himself, thus ending the lesson—

and you could be forgiven for thinking
that lesson lost until 1970 when curfew
came down hard on the Falls Road
and four were shot dead and stones
fell from a sky of building fume and

CS gas melted tears out of the eyes
of anyone watching as petrol bombs
marked the line of British soldiers
into a frieze of black and rage.

The two flanks massed and simmered.
Nothing was resolved and nothing
was made clear until 3,000 women
with their children marched up
the Falls and crossed that barricade
carrying nothing but bags of groceries.

Groceries. So maybe the stories
are wrong. Maybe Goliath walked
that sun-withered wash toward
David in hope of watching
his children age in peace. Maybe
Goliath was the ox-soft heart led
to slaughter for a new God who
shone alone like vengeance
in the heavens. Maybe Delilah
was the wine Samson was forbidden,
fruit of her, scent of ripe and union,
scent of clay and decay and sex
and peat that rises up from hillsides
here seamed by wall and rill.
Scent of two people coming
together to make a third as the rain
falls, smoothing the land to a shabby
fabric of stone and whin and cloud,
softening of the sky against which
those cranes stand, empty, like stitches
holding the patchwork greenery together.

for Zev Trachtenberg

Silence

When Ruan Pienaar lines up the kick, his eyes down
towards the small parcel he is trying to deliver
over the posts and into the heart of the south,
his thin, handsome face its own arena of concentration,
the pub goes hushed, a few hard *shushes* silencing
the chatter of those not paying enough attention
and now we are quiet as churchmen waiting to sing
our own hymn to the ball and the foot and the muscled
shoulder—"Stand Up for the Ulstermen"—waiting
to sing with our pints raised high, waiting in a deep
silence despite the fact the match happens away
across the Irish Sea, across history with its small
daily galas; we go silent as a field of grass before
a thicket of storm drops down over the Antrim Hills,
wind in the whin suddenly gone and off another way,
silent as the streets past the gasworks at two am,
silent as the Lagan canal and the linen mill, everyday
now as of a Sunday, broken windows like a brittle web
of damage that holds it all together, silent as Ravenhill;
we go as silent as we will, a few hours later,
after the match is over and Ulster has lost again,
when the young woman and her lover pick up
the pieces of a song that says love will conquer hate,
as if the two were teams opposed on a great pitch,
and play for each other, the man's hands stroking notes
out of the fiddle he rests beneath the shag of hair
he wears atop his glasses, the woman's voice settling
like a bird on each note before it rises into the pub's silence,
its arc like the arc of the rugby ball, lifting and lifting
into the long cobalt of dusk before it finally curves
away, missing the goal in a silence like the silence
that must have blossomed after the bomb went off
here in the Rose and Crown, a space that was suddenly
and forever six voices quieter, but that was years and years ago
and we have long since decided not to speak of such things.

STYLES OF HELL:

a sequence

...you must descend. It is one of the styles.

~ Larry Levis

1. In the Convento di San Francesco, Fiesole, Italy, on the 10th Anniversary of the Invasion of Iraq

Above Firenze where the light in turns
takes on the color of lavender in urns
above the Piazza Mino and aged-gray,
Etruscan walls break through hillsides
of boxwood and bay as spires of cyprus
echoing the clocktower thrust through
gardens cultivated into a permanence
of orchid and wisteria, sprayed blessings
of pastel roses throttling the masonry,
at the bottom of a stepladder staircase
below the cloisters, you will find hell.

Not Dante's murderous burned alive
in a river of fire—*that stream of blood*
where those who injure others violently,
boil—but rather paintings that depict
a Chinese hell where demons-turned-
bureaucrat preside over peasants
exactly arranged for punishment, as if
horror were not in abuse but rather
in its orchestration. Not the scourging
demon stripping flesh from a man's back
with a whip of live cats, but a gentleman
pouring tea beneath a pagoda as women
wait in line to be churned into mince
by hell's waterwheel. Another forced
to count a perpetuity of passing insects
led to diners at eternal tables overflowing
in a hell without glowing weeps of flame
consuming flesh reborn each night.

The Franciscans arrived in Beijing
in 1590 to bring an Empire into the fold
of the lamb, but for a culture that feared
the methodical more, the traditional
torments of hell read like opium

dreams. Chinese style was the long
mind of the Emperor made of mandarins
and a tectonic shifting of paper smothering
their lives the way the resistance fighter
is devoured by the paperwork of the state.

So on the posters, up to bloated demons
behind their desks, come an eternity
of souls in the everdusk waiting to be
assigned severance. Onc hoards acres
of forms and another walks hell's thickets
with a clipboard and a lamp. A third
documents each cup of tea offered up
to women this close to becoming paste.
This is the style that becomes us now,
in the fresh garden of a new century,
where our task is to watch and
record those so precisely ransacked
in the luxuriant, civil-service of torture,
to watch and record, saying nothing.

Back above in my life, in the world where
gardens mark the boundaries of paradise,
smell of lavender and poppies blooming
like spattered tenderness—after all
this time—I have climbed into an orchard
of buddleias and ash, like Orpheus
back in his grove of oaks. I have tried
to find my way out, but what is once seen
cannot be otherwise and the trees
no longer have ears. Words of the dead
loiter in the air. This night's garden lies
heavy with their style beneath a paper sky,
the inked-in shadows, and distant light
dwindling into the bloody river of sunset.

2. Jacob's Ladder, Bath, England

Dodimedis has lost two gloves. He asks that the person who
has stolen them should lose his mind and eyes in the temple.

~ curse written on a stone offered
  to the mother-goddess & recovered
  from the Bath thermal springs.

When Jacob lay down that night he placed a rock beneath his head—
fleeing Esau as he was, bereft and without succor below the racing

chariot of the sky—slept and dreamt of ladders and angels
and years and days, dreamt of stairs and the sway between heaven

and earth and when Jacob awoke from his sleep he said, *Surely*
the Lord is in this place; and I did not know it, and named

that land Beth'el.
                            But in Bath—
Roman town of golden stone and iron-hot water where curses

carved on rocks were cast into springs in the hope of the goddess's
revenge, namesake town for one in Maine where once on the rocky

accumulation of the shore I found a small stone with PROFOUND
        HURT
written across it in dark Sharpie—
                                        in Bath, the angels Jacob dreamed
clamber ladders on the façade of the Abbey toward statues

of Paul and Peter and sunset fires that limestone to flame,
the sun unbuckling the horizon's belt of cloud. Beth'el means

the house of God, and Bath was named for healing waters, but
the sky here is heavy as sediment (no nest of angels treed among

cirrus) and when someone casts a stone into the water asking for
the clarity of pain she feels to be brought down upon another

for a change, she is asking for the labor of angels to be delivered—

that dangerous interchange between heaven and earth
that rarely ends well for our all too human world—

asking for the goddess who lives in water and stone to give back
a piece of herself to one, bereft and without succor, alone

and dreaming on a rocky shore, who hopes for someone else
to be run down by the chariot of the lord for once,

and who will not know it, days or centuries later,
when the water returns that prayer, unanswered and forgiven.

3. Ye Olde Trip to Jerusalem, Nottingham, England

In the light that knifed through a thin window, I sit with a pint and a plate of cheese at a pub called the Trip whose name doesn't mean that exactly, but rather the opposite, because in the Middle Ages *Trip* meant not a journey but a resting place where journeys could be broken, and so this Trip means the way soldiers would stop for ale and kidneys beneath the castle with sunlight streaking beeches above the stableyard, a pause where swallows rest above men playing skittles down a long strip of lawn where Richard the Lionheart left once for war and a holy land he imagined and lost.

Today, *Ye Olde Trip* means an ancient public house carved into cliffs of sandstone and fern and small trees latched on to any hold they can find on the sheer cliff-edge of the world as Spring returns to England slowly. It means a pub beneath a castle where in a niche in the stone walls the *cursed galleon* rests. The *cursed galleon* is a small model of a sailing ship heavy with years of dust and grime, all the wear of history and age and repetition, a toy ship left uncleaned for so long because, the story goes, quick death alighted on anyone who dared wash it of its past.

And so while I eat, I imagine the ridiculous, untimely deaths I might bring down upon myself if I were brave enough to clean the galleon of its history. I start with cholera easy as unwashed lettuce, but on I travel and run into the abutment of bridges and drown quickly as a kitten in an over-turned boat, tumble down stairs narrow as the question mark my neck turned into on landing and hemorrhaged into my hands from a fall across a rake with the fire-laced riot of autumn spread around me—and all the while, in a corner above the bottles' crenellations, television from America displays a photo of a boy in a hood like a wanted poster, dark shadows on his face like heavy dust of the past, and the news anchor reports how he was chased through the deepwood of a subdivision and killed by a man convinced he was sheriff in his own private neighborhood of fear.

If *Ye Olde Trip* means history articulated in the way roads
here are named for Maid Marian and Friar Tuck, it also
means we remember the elegance of Sherwood where
sunlight filigrees gothic tangles of limbs in a canopy of
generous outlaws and ignore the major oak strung with
lanterns of hung men. It means we believe the Lionheart
walking out from the mist of myth to establish order,
rather than the real, French-speaking Richard, who
stripped and flogged those who came unasked to his
coronation, people who dared go where they were not
welcome until fires touched inside the lowest of clouds
above their homes and blood left their bodies to paint the
thatch and shoddy glamour of this kingdom.

This boy, perhaps, hoped he was free of the past when he
walked home through that subdivision beneath the
streetlights pooling white across the asphalt, but I should
know better. It is easy for me. This morbid imaginarium
of my possible deaths was all in fun, but I never thought
once, thinking back on it now, that I might be torn down
by a lion-heart of a man with nothing to fear but a boy in a
hood with a handful of Skittles inside the small dark ship of
a Florida night.

for Trayvon

4. Archeology

Up landfill hill where the groundwater seeps
at the base of the mound have long turned to
mud-red rainbows of iron and oil with the dog
early and below us the snow holds on in avenues
through the still bare trees, snow made ice
by passing feet and shadow as the grass nearby
sheer waits for Spring with a kind of patience
the dog doesn't share.
                                    She sprints across the field
and toboggans into cold puddles atop this pile
of trash grassed over and made marketable
for the subdivision nearby. Below the trees,
galaxy of redwings and fairy houses children
build beneath boreal oaks, dwellings of discards,
sticks and moss and roofs of purple tiles made
from mussel shells dropped by gulls onto the rocks
by the river to break them open and reveal bodies
of orange and glue.
                                    She sprints and sleds
on her shoulder across the hard ground and
into gathering pools of old snow and rain
that has nowhere to go but down, down and
through into this warren of then, down into this
mound of covered-over-and-turned-to-a-field-
where-one-might-walk-with-a-dog-some-day-
in-early-Spring. Down into the midden of our
discards—tricycles, refrigerators, oilcans, drums,
newspapers, glass and the false limb of a man
abandoned, alone with its leather straps. A horse's
skeleton approaching the flatness of fossils.
That old Ford no one could start. Two guys
shoved it to the top of the road that
led to the cliffs above the empty quarry
this hill was once, released the brake,
and watched the slow caterwaul of metal
as it tore itself apart trying to find bottom.

5. El Café a la Esquina de Agua y Vida, Seville

At the café at the corner of Water and Life
in the plaza of blood oranges at the bend
of the whitewash and archways of old stone,
between the congregation of traffic and
the soft hammers of the cathedral bells,
near baths made by Peter the Cruel and
alongside the tiny carapaces of smartcars
hived in the old Jewish quarter where
the exhausted piss-whiff of the city
wanders off into the Jardines de Murillo
where fists of palms and geometric rigmarole
circle the fountain—ficus and terra cotta frescoes
of the Christian everlasting: the gold leaf,
the halo, Madonna adoring—near the dead-end
of the road of death, beneath keyhole arches
at the mark of midyear and in the shadow
of el Real Alcázar (layered cathedral of all
that's holy here—Christian on Muslim
on Roman on something far older), where
wings of the canopy angle out to hide me
from the wallop of the noonday sun in the square
where I'm sipping a vinho verde that tastes
of the effervescence of granite and hot grass,
the woman at the public fountain, with an ache
and a fine delicacy, runs damp hands through
her spray of dark hair, sops the hot arch
of her neck, and trails fingers down her bare
arms the way Christ might have washed
Magdelane had he been a just bit more human.

6. Helen in Troy in Flames

When Menelaus enters her
chamber, his sword drawn
and erect and ready to kill
her, his hand already bloody
with the last smears of
Deiphobus, she turns
from the mirror where
she has long watched herself
run combs through
that startling wheat field
of her hair and stands
to face him with one hand
at the clasp on her shoulder.

When Menelaus enters her
chamber, he makes
the room smaller now
that he is here to fill it
with the unborn child
of his anger, the way
the Achaeans filled
the startling horse
that dyed the windswept
Trojan beach with ruin,
the horse Helen stroked
with her delicate hands,
calling to each man
inside in a throaty purr
as they curled up
in the pregnant dark.

When Menelaus enters her
chamber Helen stands
to face him with one hand
on the clasp at her shoulder.
She releases it to expose
her bare breasts
and the cloth slides off
like the river Evrotas
overflowing banks buff
with olives and into fields
of winter wheat beyond
the walls of Sparta,
far away, where Menelaus
once again drops to his knees
in silence and will not rise.

7. With Flowers

ou est elle la mort? toujours future ou passée?

My son and I stood beneath the sign,
Arrêté—C'est ici L'Empire de la mort,
and, then beneath massive lions and

the swirl of traffic about Montparnasse,
like Dante and a thirteen-year-old Virgil,
we dropped down into hell. The story

began slowly—starting with the technique
of excavation itself, how this city beneath
the city was constructed, tunnels emptied

and stone raised from dark quarries
in the fields to assemble the city of light above—
and to cemeteries emptied in the old town

and all the bones carted here: six million
bones in the long tunnels beneath Paris,
bones piled like city walls topped with

crenellations of skulls, long fencing of bone
after bone, bones and the green felt of moss
gentling the faces of these citizens.

But in a monument
to comrades lost beneath a cave-in
like a sudden folding of hands after

a day of long labor, tunnel workers carved
a façade of the *Quartier de Cazerne*
into an alcove of one shaft, a classic portico

and the scalloped archways of their home
like the castle of the poets Dante found
in hell—seven gates and beyond a meadow,

fresh and green. Back in the world above,
at *Au Bouquet*, Julian and I ate a late meal
in the February sunlight that tunneled

through the cloud-cover: vin rouge and
chocolate chaud, charcuterie and cheese
like the rough fruit of the earth itself.

as trees rooted up into that flint-
colored sky and traffic hummed past
on the Boulevard Saint-Jacques.

8. From Tarifa, Spain

Near the edge of the continent, wind turbines line lion-colored hillsides like a farm for a strange genus of sunflowers that churn and spin already this morning as the sun rises on the Atlantic, cobalt this hour and topped with a lace of waves and an Africa behind it. I am driving north to Seville from a headland and a town where commerce begins on the continent and profit was made into language because in Tarifa someone realized the inevitable—that he could charge a *tariff* for the use of his docks to ships crossing the oceans that surrounded the world then.

I am driving north to meet a translator, a man who will take my book of poems about birds of great color and war and the wet green of the landscapes of the American rainforest and turn those pages into the dry wind and sage and sunlight of his *Castellano*, and I scan the radio for a hint of music that doesn't evoke the wild rumpus of the dance hall this early on a Wednesday in April, just days after Good Friday when I watched Nazarenos descend corkscrew streets to the river carrying crosses and the chariot of the lord in agony.

They dressed in purple robes and black *capirotes*, like drag queens of the Klan, and I descended with them into the grotto of a town built into hanging cliffs of limestone along rio Trejo where willows along the cliffside flanked the ancient winehouses with their whips of new green. I descended with the procession of soldiers and children and men in wild robes like I was part of a crowd calling death down on a man under the red banners of Rome that draped from balconies where women watched, uninterested and unaware of the particular history that passed below their feet. The way they would have once ignored the specific detail of a man who carried his own cross down a road paved with jeers, down coiled streets and smaller out to the city walls and a hill called Golgotha.

In the car, the radio stumbles until it comes upon a station in Arabic and I listen to a vital discussion of nothing I understand. All I can hear is chuff and glottal stops from across this narrow sea. Words from a continent beginning in the rise of the Rif mountains and spreading across deserts and into the wind and sun and meadows of wild flowers spangled like stars on a field of green. I listen to the raw news of the world and understand nothing. It is just a wild spiral of information streaming in the stunned blue of the sky.

I listen for a long time to all this business—untranslated and current as fresh history—as all the while the arroyos cut grooves into the side of the earth along the road where I pass in my car and the green smoke of the olive trees holds their banks together. I listen to a story of past and present twined together in a rough rope like all the starlings that scatter and gather in the air above the turbines, a conversation of wing and wind, a voice that trails off into static as mile by mile I descend an undulating helix of road across hills the color of skulls.

for Jose de Maria Romero Berea

9. The Arab Baths in Ronda

If you have not seen the day of Revolution in a small town
where all know all...and always have known all,
you have seen nothing.

       ~ Hemingway

Although once through the precise retina of stars sunlight slipped
into the arched ceiling in the steam room where men sat and chin-

wagged and watched slaves fan steam from juniper fires through
four pairs of horseshoe porticoes below brick barrel vaults,

they really aren't Arab. All this is Roman, a style lost in the fall
of one empire and returned in the conquest of Iberia,

part of the understrata we walk on because the world is old
and full of stories, the way towns here are named *de la Frontera*

because they were—frontier between north and south, Roman
and barbarian, then Arab and Christian, and then Fascist

and Republican, each side carrying the small particulars
of half an empire in a collection of haversacks. Away at home,

in Belfast, my son is fighting in the school we've sent him to,
with all the easy cruelty and conviction of youth and the rain
    comes down

without its usual mercy as he steps from our flat in his uniform
each morning—tie and suit coat where a red Welsh dragon squirms

like a thin and tangled river on the breast. He carries America
with him, my son, and his small town back home like a sack

across his back that no longer protects him from the rain
or the ache of being thirteen in a country of new syllables

and old enemies, and so I have had to tell him that the town
he left hasn't forgotten the small spring flower of his life

and moved on into its own deep summer, but that, of course,
is a lie. We lose the world we leave behind when we cross that
    bridge,

like the one built atop the old aqueduct that collapsed into
the Guadalevín's thin trickle years ago, and where, in 1936,

Republican farmers chucked 500 fascists into the gorge below
as a young man named Ernest watched and worked it into story.

It's Easter holiday and we walk the old city's plazas of oranges
and white-wash and the bells after a lunch of oxtail, *queso y
    jamón ibérico,*

and a bottle of tempranillo like the nectar of smoke and sweaty
    leather,
down to the gate where sunlight breaks the brick ceiling of cloud.

We descend down the cobbled lane below walls built up century
by stone by century in hope of stopping an army, each soldier

arriving with a small bundle of fire and a knife. We walk down
    the path
leading onward atop broken frontiers and constellations of
    flagstone

to the baths that aren't Arab and a past that isn't, down
to *Arroyo de las Culebras* where the slither of the river disappears

into the canyon—long shaft of willow and bulwark of stone
and stone and shadow that divides the city, old from new,

rain sealing all the riprap together in the end.

10. Sleeping Through It

When the tree came down
across the fence in the night
and blustered its barky limbs
across the small lawn
and missed our bedroom
by inches, I heard only
the mute swan of my own sleep.
When I was asked to attend
the convening of the committee
on safety's evanescence,
I was hard at work adjusting
the machinery of silence.
When traffic spun past weaving
its dangerous cloth of taillights
and the light on the corner
flashed its amber Morse,
I listened to the unending
echoes of rocks in the canyon
of quiet. When the fires
of July erupted and the night
smelled of burned rubber
and oil, I was carefully
unaware of the tiny openings
of the stars. When jackdaws
belted their minor key lament,
like a low smoky chuff
in the dark, when
planes blinked across
an upturned bowl called
the sky, when happiness
and sorrow demanded
my attention,
I was memorizing
the language of hush.
When the muster of names
was shouted out and
my presence was required,

I slept on at the mercy
of the flowers in the apple
orchard as they blossomed
into moths made of white
like the ash of bodies burned on
ghats along the holy river of night.

§

Elegy with Penelope & a Vineyard in it

I need to rewrite a story. I need to unweave
the whole war, raise up the burning tower,

shuttle heroes back across the sea through the warp
of the waves. I must pull the wind back

into its gold sack.
                  To tell it all, I need to bring up Dionysus,
god of the smashed grape, unraveler, my friend in the night

as the suitors grumble & fuss & ride each other in their sleep,
legs thrown about like logs.
                        I need to tell you how it began:

§

in a short slant of sunlight on a table in the kitchen
a man works his poems in the slow arithmetic of days

rotating towards winter, in a room above life accumulating
in the rooms below & below him, below me,

as the suitors gather like goats & the harvest assembles
in the woven silos to feed them all as the fire smudges

itself out in the afternoon before it is built again for the evening
meal—in all this it began. I arrived at Ajax

in a courtyard laid out across the enormous carpet
of his shadow, & those walls the soldiers writhe

over, fires sparking in the temples like woven stars
I cannot wait to unravel. Earth all around tamped down

by the ruckus of feet, earth tamped down like brown
sugar tamped down, flame stroking the spoon.

In the sweep of my weaving I arrived
at Ajax and could go no further,

§

here's the other half of the story: Dionysus tilts out
from inside the olives trees & offers a farmer something new,

something the world has been waiting for without knowing it.

He augers holes in a dried riverbed, plants vines wiry
as old men. He blesses the earth with a spray of piss.

Dionysus dances his little ox-foot dance and he hoes some weeds.
The farmer watches with one-eye on his daughter,

one eye on the shaggy androgyny rambling through his fields
as the vineyard thickens into old men gripping each others' shoulders &

the grapes gather in the crush. They break & juice
like small burst suns.   Not long after, this man with his poems,

§

this Larry Levis, reads to a small crowd in an abandoned dormitory.

His baggy jacket & Ned Flanders mustache, the upturned
chin & slouch at the podium as he bends into the page.

Floor lighting paints a colossal shadow on the wall behind him.
He offers his poems like glasses of wine, deep swallows

of crimson, in each poem the moment held perpetually
aloft like those same glasses before they touch,

which is the image of our trust in one another,

which is the way Dionysus & the farmer get drunk together:
dust, olives & the long light of the setting sun,

the two of them around the fire. They tip the small hearts
of the wine pouches to their mouths & drain them. Then

the farmer's daughter arrives & wonders just what her dad
is up to now. They get *her* drunk & no one has any idea

what that means yet, just as no one knows I am now dismantling

the scene of Ajax's madness in the garden, unthreading
the slaughtering of the sheep as the suitors sleep on

in the hush of the great hall. The three of them clatter beneath
     the stars
& bang through the orchard

wearing cooling jars as hats—slaves bark their fear into the night—
all of them drunk & stumbling. Now

§

Larry Levis is shaking my hand & the hand
of everyone in the dormitory with all its empty rooms

sleeping overhead. He is saying something kind

& elemental;
                    I want to say more about this moment,
but there is nothing more to say as I slipped out from the line

& let the next one hear something kind & elemental, imperfect
as words are imperfect, as the threads of this story

spill in imperfect piles at my feet.

No one said anything about the farmer & his daughter,
no one said anything about the goat that was eating the leaves

of the vines as we opened the doors & wandered into the broad quiet
of a Midwestern night. The farmer will skin the goat that dared

to eat his vines with a long knife.
He will open the animal & let the entrails spool around his feet.

He will wear its moist pelt, dance the first tragedy with his goat feet
& as he does something vast begins.

He dances his feet into hooves & his head into horns.

he dances his pride & his age, the small field of white
he's cultivating at his temples. He dances his life &

57

he dances his death that is arriving without a sound in the flexing
    leaves.
He dances & the dance *around* the goat becomes the dance of
    the goats,

& slowly what was the goat began to be replaced by what was
    not the goat;
thus the poem is made from what is not poetic, the song

from what is not worth singing. Now he stalks past the Blue Note,
a little drunk, the crowd spreading into the broad quiet of a
    Midwestern night.

Now he smells the vinegar & lines up the needle
as Ajax in his shame lines up his sword to dive on it.

I am just now banishing that moment from the fabric.

§

The farmer takes his ox cart & trundles around, showing off his vine,
pouring wine skins dark as hearts for shepherds

who drink & feel for the first time fuzzy around the eyes,
tongues sloshing in their mouths. They have been waiting

for this looseness, this easy laughter around the fire.
They have been waiting without knowing it,

which is a kind of waiting, but they don't know that either. So
when the moment comes they bring to it suspicion, the lightest
    of emotions, &

an anger which weighs them down. In the image of rumor,
    of how we cannot, finally,
trust each other, all the shepherds take a turn dividing him:

one with a rock, one with a sickle, one with an axe, one with a hoe.

They circle him, & their ululations ring off the clouds
as their arms drop out of the dark above the fire,

his dance becomes their dance, his blood
becomes their wine.

§

It's his body the daughter finds in a trench below
the orchard after Dionysus has punted off to other fields.

It's his body she climbs as she rungs up into the tree

made of grief where she'll be found in the morning swinging
back & forth, back & forth between the axis

of what is meant and what is said,

between the two hearts that keep beating inside the body of
    this story—
the soft iambic of pulsing blood that becomes

a thread of wine spooling on the floor.

I would place Ajax, back in his health, standing colossal
before all the Trojan spearmen, his shadow thrown against

the great wall but now all the threads are tangled;

now he is reading from "Caravaggio: Swirl and Vortex,"
now he is planting vines.

I can stack the past like bottles of green glass chalked
with small white numerals,

I can unweave myth & fact back into the cabinets
where they are stored, packed like spools,

but something remains in the threads
even as they run down around my feet.

The Rolling Stones Visit the Cave of Hercules, 1967, Morocco

The Stones arrived, the guidebook says, amid
drug busts and the band starting to split,
at this cave where Hercules rested

after separating Africa from Europe, shoving
the gates of Gibraltar apart and watching
the stunned flood of whales pass between

his legs, this cave where Berbers for years
worked millstones from the walls for grinding
olives and left unfinished discs stamped

in the basalt, grooved like gold records hung
in offices across London.   When the band
washed up in Tangiers with *kif* and hash

and the silver moons of necklaces they wore,
they trundled through streets busy with the smell
of bread baked in *ferranes* up to the Kasbah

and the Café HaHa with the sound of jajouka
in the middle distance (smatter and bash
of the cymbals and hand drums and goat pipes

tooling up) in a city where the streets narrow to arms
against the sky and the phantasmagoria of the souks.
In this cave Hercules was becoming something

that the world had never seen—half-man,
who would live forever in the afterlife of the stars—
but now he was tired. He had schlepped

his way through the zodiac of his labors
and thought he was nearly done (only a garden
at the end of the world remained, with a sky

that needed to be held aloft) and there was nothing
left for him, he thought, just a chamber
carved out of rock where he could bundle

the skin of his lion and finally lay down his head,
just as Mick and the boys recline by the pool,
out of the sun, waiting for the labor

they don't know is coming—the banquet
and the quagmire of their four legendary albums,
the harrowing of the streets, the sticky, brown-

sugar, death-in-the-eyes quartet that ends
in the perfect blue garden of *Exile on Main Street*—
and smoking a hookah as Brian Jones falls apart

and Keith absconds with Anita like Pan seducing
the moon. The gift of music was given away
in this cave by a half-man, half-goat who was perhaps

only a boy wrapped in a goat's skin who stumbled
out from the edge of the darkness and began his dance
as the flutes and guitars and the swiveling drums

all started talking at the same time like Keith and Brian
playing for the last time together on "Midnight Rambler,"
that whomp of the blues harp and Keith's guitar knocking

the backbeat. The boys walk through the Kasbah
with the smell of that bread floating ahead of them
like fame as the song of the muezzin ripples out

beyond the city, arabesques ringing the open green door
of the mosque, the door that resembles the mouth
of a cave where discs are cut and grooved and

the world is only a distant melody of strife
to a workman who sleeps, his hat down across
his eyes, and waits for the afternoon's labor to begin.

Artists Sketching in the White Mountains

The *momento mori* of the dead tree
bows in the foreground of this painting
of painters in front of the white-gold gulf
of sunset as it joins the strata of darkness
lying down over mountains in layers
and draped across canvas on each easel.
Missing is the fourth painter who frames
the scene and designs this arc of artists,
back-to like three separate angels
of history. Boater hats and parasols
float above their heads like buoys
in the oceanic dusk. The one painter
whose bag of paints lies before him
like a flag, full semaphore; he alone
sees the gull in the late light tossed
like a ketch on a heavy sea. He sees
the wrack and jetsam of stumps
the other painters do not, the broken
land turned up before the plow, white
pines flowing down to the coast in rivers
for masts and timbers out onto the sea.

The Giant's Ring

Bronze Age henge tomb, Ballynahatty

I rode a rented bike out the towpath
to the Giant's Ring that day in April,
but it was horses that raced this circle
of mounded earth larger than a circus tent
one hundred years ago. Three thousand
and this henge rang with torchlight
and silence as the living circled round
to watch the dead ascend into myth astride
the imagined horses of the dark. Time
engraves everything with loss and what
little remains—stones in a crumbling
passage tomb balanced at the point of ruin—
blends with all that comes behind. Across
patterned fields falling away toward
the slow smear of the Lagan and rising up
again beyond the rain, the day played out
its normal drama—wind and the sudden
transformation of the sunlight breaking
through a roil of murky cloud—the world
alive in a smolder of Spring sky as if inside
the walls the dead assembled and ghostly
horses raced in a cavalcade of froth
and stirrup six times around the ring—
parasols and boater hats floating above
spectators ascending into heaven
on the clouded breath of their own cheers.

Rain, or a local poet long gone returns home

The lightning bangs and the rain takes its cue
and looses its sacks of stones across my spring-
cleared roof, but I hear another night in another city
when rain rushed down as never before—a night
in Belfast when poets read into the rising atrium
of the Ulster Museum and rain was shrapnel
on a steel roof, rain was horses in a galloping dark,
the audience marooned there in that tower of art
and history—soaring pterodactyl crossing space
above our heads, Irish wolfhound hugely in the corner,
posters acknowledging the Troubles down the hall—
as the main lights vanished and the fingers
of emergency lighting pointed out faces in the crowd
while heavy shoulders of thunder kept us trapped
in that bamboo garden of rain that fell and fell
all around us and the rain kept coming and coming
and water flowed feet deep down Botanic
and flooded cars all along that street of bookshop
and pub, the chip shop's lights like a ship lost at sea,
until there was nothing to do but retire to the pub
across the street beneath a rain that fell like
tenacity and the weight of history that lives on
and filled Friar's Bush graveyard across from the pub—
stone-bound acre of tall grass and headstones thin
as roofing slates where the fake 'Friar's Stone' found
inside and inscribed *AD 485* is, in fact, Victorian affection
for a gothic past of mist and myth, because back then
everyone was trying to forget the bodies dead
from cholera and famine in 1847 when the island
was wet with death and the thin arms of the starving
beneath another rain that gathered like an accumulation
of syntax and the long layering of grammar
and history and hatred and dogged abandonment,
and people either left or died, which is the condensed history
of this island, and the easy answer, and wrong, because
someone had to stay behind, someone had to write it

all down, someone had to catalogue this space
made empty by rain: green land of stone and rill
and the vandalized sheep, small back room of an island
now dark and filled with chatter and pints,
a peat fire burning ancient, heaped accumulations,
and these bodies warming, ridding themselves of the rain.

for Marianne Boruch

Surfing Dunfagnaghy: Donegal, Ireland

In Sheephaven Bay the waves line up
like corduroy—fabric of kings—
and the clouds colonnade and fill
with a light clean and well-traveled,
come as it does across the reaches
of the dark the way the wind carries
across the Atlantic, shoving the water
before it, building it and piling it
until it resembles the inevitable and
its own weight crumbles and the long
slide toward equilibrium begins.
Each wave wears itself out as it
reaches for the wrack at the back
of the shore.   I am a small darkness
in the water, a neoprene thing
that bobs and waits for the moment
to quicken and the brawny heartbeat
of the water to rise up behind me,
the thrust of it threading up the vein
of the narrowing bay—Rosguill
and Horn Head on either arm,
the green insignia of their fields
marked off in in the ancient stone
patterns of family and clan—until
the wave hits me and lifts.
                                 Suddenly
I am above the water and its rhythm,
sliding along the green wall as if
free from all history and its burly
carriage, everything from the land
that descends at last to the water.
But that is not now. Now, I am
a small stillness in an endless
weave, waiting for something

to happen, because such effort
is timing and patience in pursuit of
a moment, riding not water but
a pulse that leaves the water behind.

for Kate Miles

Smack Daniel's Band Plays Reggae at the Colle Ameno, Pontecchio Marconi, Italy

As Chad drops the beat on a trash can and Vonn kicks cats out of the shadows with the sound of his bass, we're drinking prosecco in the heat on out the deck of the *osteria* built among the ruins of an old villa where the Germans, trying to hold on to the last tatters of the Gothic line in 1944, separated the men who couldn't work from the boys who could and filled a grave with them.

Grasshoppers in the poppies buzz like speaker feedback as the band muscles into "I Shot the Sherriff." Vonn squawks, *If I am guilty I will pay*, as Scott tosses wah-wahs into the corners of a chapel long since converted to other lives: communal houses and laundry turned semaphore on lines where it's long dry.

Beyond the gate old walls fall in on themselves in an elegant wreckage that becomes something else here beneath the sun thudding on this deck, the renovated world that wants desperately to construct something from the past's bucket of wrack and girder.

Now there are plates of hard goat cheese like a sharp and wonderful chalk, salamis fat and greased, and an apricot-colored pinot grigio like the ripe fruit of sunlight and stone. Now there is dancing and the make-shift band stumbles through the intro of "War," stops, starts again and then finds their way through the song as if following a trail made long ago up a hillside of green timber and dry grass.

It's always this way. Happiness I mean. The day's heat is strong and fresh, the wine tastes of jasmine and history, we believe, lies a long way away.

for John and Chad

For the Blind Man in the Basilica di Santa Croce, Florence

Our stories can only carry us so far. I know
there are layers beneath the layers and
you haven't asked but I would describe
a fresco not even finished in the workshop,
discovered beneath damaged plaster here
in the *Scuola del Cuoio*. A simple Madonna
and child marked off with a draftsman's
patience, a sketch of faces each etched
with a different kind of cross. Evidence
of a man working out art's proportions
like a map in the sand: golden mean
in the plaster and articulation balanced
between the bridge in the distance
for scale and the sketched-in step-child
abandoned almost in the foreground,
clutching at the mother's skirts—all
the necessary work that gets covered over
in the finish, smoothed out and blessed
with plaster and color, that blinding light
cast by the angelic child, mother adoring.
I would describe it all—but that's easy
and I am not so foolish anymore. I know
you don't need me to tell you this.
You know the chittering of swallows as
they fill the courtyard of the cloister and
the weight of sunlight on cypress and stone.
If meaning is made of anything you will
have heard it in the sound of great space
that flows down the stairs of the Pazzi chapel,
in the rattle of the tourist dragging
his bag on the pavers as he moves toward
enormous doors flung open into the heat.

Notes

Led Zeppelin Debuts "Stairway to Heaven," Ulster Hall, March 5, 1971:

Belfast was blitzed by two hundred bombers of the German Luftwaffe on April 15, 1941. Apart from London, this attack represented the greatest loss of life in any night raid during the Blitz. A large number of US servicemen were stationed in Belfast at the time of the raid. Those dancing at Ulster Hall that night were not allowed to leave until the bombing ceased.

The New Faces of Belfast:

The Shankill Butchers were an Ulster loyalist (Protestant) gang responsible for as many as 23 sectarian murders between 1972-79.

Certain things here are quietly American:

The title is the opening line of one of the sections of Derek Walcott's book-length poem, *Midsummer*.

Man vs. Wild:

The video my son produced is viewable here: www.youtube.com/watch?v=mnlIu7mSrkU

Stroke City:

The controversy over the name of Derry/Londonderry is deep and goes back to the Plantation of Ulster, when the English brought Presbyterian Scots into northern Ireland to control the last of the autonomous Irish. My ancestors were among them. The plantation model of colonization was then re-used in the Americas.

The Pyre in Holywood:

On Eleventh Night (the evening proceeding July the 12th) massive bonfires are lit in Protestant neighborhoods across Northern Ireland in commemoration of the Glorious Revolution and the victory of William of Orange at the Battle of the Boyne.

The Mona Lisa of Belfast:

> The Mona Lisa of Belfast is a famous protestant mural in Lower Shankill that depicts a UFF officer pointing a rifle directly at the viewer. It was demolished on August 20th, 2015. The phrase *Quis separabit?* is the motto of, among others, the Ulster Defense Association and means *Who will separate us?*

In the Convento di San Francesco, Fiesole, Italy, on the 10th Anniversary of the Invasion of Iraq:

> Quotes from Canto XII of Dante's *Inferno*.

Elegy with Penelope and a Vineyard in It:

> Is dedicated, obviously I hope, to Larry Levis and uses variations on several sentences from Roberto Calasso's remarkable book *The Marriage of Cadmus and Harmony.*

Artists Sketching in the White Mountains :

> Is after the painting by Winslow Homer

JEFFREY THOMSON is a poet,
memoirist, translator, and editor,
and is the author of multiple books
including the memoir *fragile*, the
poetry collection *Birdwatching in
Wartime*, *The Complete Poems of
Catullus*, and the edited collection
From the Fishouse. He has been an
NEA Fellow, the Fulbright
Distinguished Scholar in Creative
Writing at the Seamus Heaney
Poetry Centre at Queen's
University Belfast, and the Hodson
Trust-John Carter Brown Fellow at
Brown University. He is currently
professor of creative writing at the
University of Maine Farmington.